By

Phillip Rich

EKKLISIA PROPHETIC
APOSTOLIC MINISTRIES, INC.

Take note that the name satan is not capitalized. We choose not to acknowledge him, even to the point of violating grammatical rules

Table of Contents

The Prophetic Amen

2 Chronicles 20:20; *"And they rose early in the morning, and went forth into the wilderness of Tekoa: and as they went forth, Jehoshaphat stood and said, Hear me, O Judah, and ye inhabitants of Jerusalem; Believe in the LORD your God, so shall ye be established; believe his prophets, so shall ye prosper."*

The word believe is *aman* (*aw-man'*). We would pronounce it as amen. In the Hebrew it means to foster as a parent or a nurse, to be faithful to, to be permanent with, to go to the right hand of, to have a long continuance with or be established on. We are to take something that has been said and foster or nurse it. To be permanent with means you cannot be moved; you have the word. To go to the right hand means to come into covenant with that word. With that understanding, let's go back and see what this verse is really talking about.

To *believe in the Lord your God* means to come into covenant with Him and what He has said. It means to be permanent with it, to foster

1

/nurse what He has said. That means to birth it, to bring it from the spirit realm into the natural realm. You stay with that word until it happens. You are established in it.

Believe His prophets means the same thing. We are to believe what they are saying and come into covenant with it.

Instead of saying, "*If this is of God, we will see. We will put it on a shelf. If it is the Lord, it will come to pass. If it isn't, then it won't.*" None of that is true and is a false assumption. Let me prove it to you.

Do you believe Isaiah was a true prophet? Do you believe that everything he prophesied was of God?

Isaiah 53:4-5; *"Surely he hath borne our griefs, and carried our sorrows: yet we did esteem him stricken, smitten of God, and afflicted. But he was wounded for our transgressions, he was bruised for our iniquities: the chastisement of our peace was upon him; and with his stripes we are healed."*

That scripture is a prophecy which says we are healed. Now, how many Christians are still sick? They assume that if God said it, they don't have to do anything with it. It will automatically happen. That assumption is incorrect. You have to come into an amen with what is being said. You have to be fully persuaded, come into a covenant of permanence. "*I am not moved. God said it. I say an astounding amen to what God has said and what He has said through His prophets. I am not letting go of it. I am going to foster it and nurse it like a parent would nurse a child until it is mature and comes to pass in my life.*"

God's Prophetic Word

Are you aware that the Word of God itself is a prophecy?

1 Thessalonians 5:19-21; "*Quench not the Spirit. Despise not prophesyings. Prove all things; hold fast that which is good.*"

Quench means to extinguish it, to try and put out the fire.

The Greek word for despise is *exoutheneo* (*ex-oo-then-eh'-o*) and means to be least esteemed, to make light of a thing. In other words, you don't give it the place it deserves.

When you hear a prophecy from a true prophet of God and your spirit identifies with it, you are to esteem that word as a word from the Spirit of God to you. The Holy Spirit in you will identify with what the Holy Spirit has said. Scripture says that your spirit will bear witness. To bear witness means something clicks on the inside of you and you get a yes on the inside.

That word is supposed to be important to you. It is not supposed to be something that we can take or leave or see whether or not it is from the Lord. If I don't birth a prophetic word, then it will stay in word form forever until I take it into my heart, get pregnant with it and give birth to it in the natural.

You have to get pregnant with that prophetic word. Mary did. She said, "*Be it unto me according to the word.*" What was she saying? "*I take it into the womb of my spirit. I accept it.*" She started meditating on it, rehearsing it until she was pregnant with that Word. She carried that Word full term and gave birth to what was prophesied.

The Lord is showing us what to do with the prophetic Word of God and a prophetic word by the Spirit of God. The Word and the Spirit are in agreement. They are not opposite of each other.

Despise not Prophesying

Don't despise prophesying. Many times we have despised prophesy and not realized we did. I have because I didn't esteem it high enough, take it serious enough. I didn't realize I had a responsibility with that word to give birth to it in my spirit and bring it into the natural realm. Your spirit is the transporter from the spirit realm to the natural realm. Your spirit is the link between the heavenly realm and the earthly realm.

You must latch onto that word and hide it in your heart as Mary did. You must say, "*Be it unto me according to the word.*" Take hold of it and come into covenant with it. Do not come out of agreement or covenant with it. It will come to pass because God the Holy Spirit has said it. If you want to be the kind of person who is always seeing the prophetic words you get come to pass, this is how. The bible says a promise that is given remains. What does that mean?

When a prophecy was given to the children of Israel it loomed over their heads as a word. They wouldn't take it to heart. It was frivolous to them. There was another generation though that reached up and took the word serious. They put it in their heart and said, *"Be it unto us according to the word."* They birthed it and walked into the land of promise, the land that flowed with milk and honey. They took the promises of God and it came to pass for them. A promise remains until somebody comes into the rest of faith, takes hold of it and says an eternal amen to that word.

Be careful though to what you say amen to. Remember when you say amen in the church or someone walks up and says amen – you are saying you are in covenant with that. If someone says their headache is killing them, don't say amen. *"Oh, the devil has been after me all week."* Don't say amen to that. Always ask if they want you to come in covenant with that word. They will probably say no and change what they are saying. Make sure somebody agrees with you for the right thing.

1 Thessalonians 5:21; *"Prove all things; hold fast that which is good."*

Prove in this verse is talking about proving the prophecy.

How do you prove the prophecy? Prove means to test it, discern it, to approve of it. Your spirit and your knowledge of the Word will let you know if that word is of God. Another factor that comes into play is the person who is giving the word. Do you know if they have a track record for speaking the Word of God? Do you know if they are a true vessel of the Lord, serve God, have a prayer life, and walk with God?

Hold fast means to keep in your memory, to seize upon what was said and to possess it. Hold fast to the prophecy that you know is of God. It shocks me the number of people I have given prophetic words to and they don't remember I said it to them. I don't see these people very often and even I sometimes remember what I have said.

One of the keys is that you must esteem the word - the written Word and the word of the Spirit through a vessel. It is a form of honor to esteem that word. Whatever we honor, we attract to our life. Whatever we dishonor, we push away from our life. To not remember what God has said is a form of dishonor. Take it seriously and remember what God has said, even if it means writing it down. Taking the time to write it down means you honor it. If you honor it, you are attracting it to your life.

Good in this verse means valuable to your life.

Hold fast to a prophecy, seize upon it, remember it, and take hold of that which is valuable to your life. When you get a prophecy that you say is a great word, don't assume it is automatically going to happen.

Isaiah said that by the stripes of Jesus you are healed, but that doesn't mean you are automatically healed. We know Isaiah was a true prophet whose words are a prophecy. We have to take that word to heart, go over it, meditate on it and say, *"Be it done unto me according to the Word of God."* You have to use your faith and patience together until that promise is fulfilled.

Why do you think we have to do any differently with the prophecy of God through a man or woman of God? The church in the past has taught us wrong about prophecy.

Before we go on, let me remind you that a prophetic word is not a guarantee. It is an invitation the same way the Word of God is an invitation to a miracle. Prophecy is God's will being spoken out. It is what He would love to do for you. But, you have to embrace it.

2 Peter 1:19-21; *"We have also a more sure word of prophecy; whereunto ye do well that ye take heed, as unto a light that shineth in a dark place, <u>until the day dawn</u>, and the day star arise in your hearts: Knowing this first, that no prophecy of the scripture is of any private interpretation. For the prophecy came not in old time by the will of man: but holy men of God spake as they were moved by the Holy Ghost."*

<u>*Until the day dawn*</u> means the day it manifests. Jesus is the day star. You are going to give birth to what was prophesied. You must take heed to it, take hold of it.

These verses also tell us that scripture is prophecy. Prophecy still comes the same way today. Men and women of God are inspired by the Holy Spirit, the Spirit speaks something to them, shows them something and they speak out what the Spirit of God has given them. I am not saying prophecy should hold the identical same place in our priorities as the Word of God, but it should have a place higher than it has had. If we will take the prophecies that we have received seriously, we will see them come to pass as God has said.

I have had some great prophecies in my life that I have seen come to pass. There are others that I am birthing. Are you pregnant with a prophecy? Have you said, *"Be it done unto me according to that word?"* I did. That is my word and it is going to come to pass in my life. This is what God said by His Spirit. We almost need to cease saying, *"Prophet Phil said..."* or *"Brother so and so said..."* and begin to say, *"The Holy Spirit said..."* It comes by the Spirit of God. The Lord will use any vessel, but it is Him speaking and that should become extremely important to us.

Some of you may remember what God has said through the prophets. You might write them down, get the cds, rehearse them, go over them in your heart and in your mind. You are the ones who will see everything said come to pass. Those who have not taken it serious, can't remember what the Lord said through somebody have the potential to see it come to pass, but probably never will. That prophecy is looming in the spirit over their head waiting for them to get serious with it.

Make a decision not to despise prophesying. Prove it and hold fast to that which is good. Give birth to it and bring it from the spiritual realm into the natural realm. You need to say with your mouth, *"This word is going to manifest for me."*

Birth the Word

If you start getting serious with what the Holy Spirit has said, there will be manifestations of what the Holy Spirit has said. Are you ready for the word to become flesh in your life? There is a difference between a spoken prophetic word and a manifested prophetic word. Between those two there is something for us to do. We have to give birth to it, take hold of it and be serious with it. We must rehearse it, remember it, speak it out of our mouths. It has to have a place in our lives.

In 2 Chronicles 20 we read about a prophetic word a prophet gave that the people had to do something with. In verse 14 we read that the Spirit came upon Jahaziel, the son of the prophet Zechariah. He being prophesying to all the children of Israel.

2 Chronicles 20:15-16; *"And he said, Hearken ye, all Judah, and ye inhabitants of Jerusalem, and thou king Jehoshaphat, Thus saith the LORD unto you, Be not afraid nor dismayed by reason of this great multitude; for the battle is not yours, but God's. To morrow go ye down against them: behold, they come up by the cliff of Ziz; and ye shall find them at the end of the brook, before the wilderness of Jeruel."*

Jahaziel gave some detailed words in this prophecy. They were not just words of encouragement, but about some things they were supposed to do. They were not just supposed to sit back and let God take care of them.

The people were supposed to go down a certain way and so a certain thing. Jahaziel told the people in detail where they would find the enemy.

2 Chronicles 20:17; *"Ye shall not need to fight in this battle: set yourselves, stand ye still, and see the salvation of the LORD with you, O Judah and Jerusalem: fear not, nor be dismayed; to morrow go out against them: for the LORD will be with you."*

The word battle is the King James Version is in italics, meaning it was added by the translators.

The people were not to war over the fact that there was something for them to do or that it would not happen the way they thought it would or that there were three armies. They were not going to need to fight in those battles. They were not going to have to battle over the prophetic word. They were to accept the word and quit fighting what God had said.

Sometime God will say something to us and our flesh fights over it. *"Go down against them? There are three armies. Go to the cliff of Ziz? That is a dangerous place. Go to Zeruel? We don't want to go there."*

Don't fight the prophetic word. Embrace it.

There was a battle and a fight that they did do. They fought using praise as their weapon.

They were not to fight the prophetic word, but accept what was said. Accept what God is saying. Do what He is saying. Follow His lead. It will work for you. If God is telling you to do something, it will work for you even though you may not understand it. There is always an instruction to a miracle. Ever heard of working of a miracle? That means God will tell you to do something and when you do, then He releases a miracle.

I remember one time when I spoke to a person who needed healing in their legs. The Lord told me to have them stomp their feet. They didn't want to because their legs were hurting. They were in pain. I told them again to stomp their feet. Now before they stomped their feet, there was no healing. As they stomped their feet, healing and miracles came. There is an instruction to a miracle.

Don't fight the instruction. Go ahead and do what you are instructed to do. Every miracle has an instruction to it. There is something we are supposed to do. It might be as simple as lifting your hands and praising God. Sometimes it might be praising in the darkness of the hour. It might be forgiving somebody or going and praying for somebody else.

I heard a story about Oral Roberts. One time he was very sick. He prayed for and tried to minister to himself, but couldn't get healed. He asked the Lord what was wrong and the Lord told him to go to the hospital and pray for every sick person he could find. When he got there, the Lord directed him to people. He prayed for seven people and every one of them was healed. As soon as he ministered to the seventh person, he was completely healed. While he was praying for these people, he remarked that he thought he was sicker that some of them. They were getting healed and he was still sick. The Lord told him to keep doing it.

Just follow the instruction.

2 Chronicles 20:18; "*And Jehoshaphat bowed his head with his face to the ground: and all Judah and the inhabitants of Jerusalem fell before the LORD, worshipping the LORD.*"

The people took the prophetic word and started worshipping God. Why would you worship God over a prophetic word? Is it because you believe that word is going to come to pass for you? Do you believe the word or not? The Holy Spirit is releasing instruction to us so we can see every word God has given us come to pass.

When Elizabeth rejoiced over Mary's word, she was filled with the Holy Spirit. The babe in her womb began to leap and was filled with the Holy Spirit. Then out of the mouth of Elizabeth came a prophetic word, a prophetic anointing that was released back to Mary. All of this was based on her rejoicing over someone else's word.

Rejoice Over the Word

Start rejoicing when someone else is getting a prophetic word and that same glory that is coming on them will come all over you.

Why is rejoicing so important?

Isaiah 12:2-3; *"Behold, God is my salvation; I will trust, and not be afraid: for the LORD JEHOVAH is my strength and my song; he also is become my salvation. Therefore with joy* [rejoicing] ***shall ye draw water out of the wells of salvation."***

When I rejoice with others who are being blessed, I draw water out of the well of salvation. There are seven wells. There is a well of healing, one of deliverance, another of prosperity. Those seven wells cover the total meaning of salvation. The meaning of salvation in the Old Testament is the same as that in the New Testament. The word Jesus means salvation. He is literally everything we need.

2 Chronicles 20:21-25; *"And when he had consulted with the people, he appointed singers unto the LORD, and that should praise the beauty of holiness, as they went out before the*

army, and to say, Praise the LORD; for his mercy endureth for ever. And when they began to sing and to praise, the LORD set ambushments against the children of Ammon, Moab, and mount Seir, which were come against Judah; and they were smitten. For the children of Ammon and Moab stood up against the inhabitants of mount Seir, utterly to slay and destroy them: and when they had made an end of the inhabitants of Seir, every one helped to destroy another. And when Judah came toward the watch tower in the wilderness, they looked unto the multitude, and, behold, they were dead bodies fallen to the earth, and none escaped. And when Jehoshaphat and his people came to take away the spoil of them, they found among them in abundance both riches with the dead bodies, and precious jewels, which they stripped off for themselves, more than they could carry away: and they were three days in gathering of the spoil, it was so much."

This was a prophetic word that the people took hold of and began to act upon. They began to rejoice, worship and praise over it. Afterwards, they started collecting all the spoils.

2 Chronicles 20:26; *"And on the fourth day they assembled themselves in the valley of Berachah; for there they blessed the LORD: therefore the* *name of the same place was called, the valley of Berachah, unto this day."*

This valley is the valley of the dance and rejoicing. Whatever prophecy you can rejoice and dance over, you will get the spoil of. You can rejoice and dance before it happens because God has said it. The rejoicing over a prophecy is part of the process of birthing it. You know it is going to happen in your life. You know it is going to come to pass for you. It is a word spoken from the very Spirit of God directly into your life.

Have you ever said that a word you received was a good word? If it is a good word and it comes from God, we should want that to come to pass enough to begin to operate in faith and bring it from the spirit into the natural. When God speaks a word it is still in the spirit realm, but it is available for the womb of your spirit. It is the womb of your spirit that transfers things from the spirit into the natural. Mary got pregnant in the spirit before she ever got pregnant in the natural. She birthed that word in the spirit before she ever birthed Jesus in the natural.

Are you going to take prophecy more seriously now? It won't be a hope so, maybe so thing or wouldn't it be nice if, but a sure word of prophecy. A sure word is one that is going to come to pass. It will happen for you.

1 Timothy 1:18; *"This charge I commit unto thee, son Timothy, according to the prophecies which went before on thee, that thou by them mightiest war a good warfare;"*

A good warfare is the same thing as a good game. We hear people say it was a good game because their team won. A good game is one you are winning. A good warfare is one you are winning.

Do you know why God wants us to have prophecies? He is omniscient (all knowing), omnipresent, omnipotent (all powerful). God knows it all – past, present and future. Because He knows it all, He knows what is coming in the future for you. Therefore He will have somebody speak a word about it. It won't always be about the problem. Many times it will be about a promise that will take care of the problem. So when God says to you that He will bless you financially and increase you it could mean you are about to have a battle in your life and the devil wants to take all your finances away. But, God could say that He is going to bless you so that you take hold of that word. Then no matter what the devil says to you,

you will birth the fact that you are going to be blessed.

There are times when a prophecy will come over somebody's life about walking in health and defeating sickness because there is a battle on the way. That prophecy becomes a weapon of mass destruction against what satan has planned. God tells us what His plans are for us so that we will take hold of it, not be moved and defeat the plans of the enemy.

God has plans for you – to prosper you, give you an expected end, a hope and a future. Are you aware that satan also has a plan? It is to destroy us as Christians, to take us down. 2 Corinthians 2:11 says not to be ignorant of satan's devises lest he take advantage of you. That means if you are ignorant of how he operates, he is going to attack you and you won't have a defense. God gives us prophecies to destroy the schemes of the enemy.

I recall prophesying to one man that I saw something and didn't know if it had already happened, was happening or was about to happen to him. I told him what I saw hitting his physical body. Then I told him how to defeat the thing. He told me he was feeling fine and nothing was wrong with him. Maybe, I answered, God was giving him a word so he would know what to do. The very next day he was hit with sickness. He took the prophecy and destroyed that thing.

He came to me later and told me that if I hadn't given him that word, he would have ended up in the hospital. He took the word as a weapon and knocked that thing out.

So, prophecy can be a tremendous tool against the enemy. A prophetic word will keep you alive and raise you from the dead. One missionary had a prophecy about his son being a mighty minister of the gospel. The son died and was laid out in a pine box. The missionary opened the box and proclaimed the word of the Lord was that his son would preach the gospel. When he said that, his boy began to take deep breaths and came back to life. This was done with a prophetic word.

A prophetic word will keep you alive. A prophetic word will raise you from the dead. It will give you an advantage over demonic spirits. It will cause you to have a place of ascendency over the enemy, walking in great victory if you understand the power of it and what God is trying to do.

Don't turn lose of what God has said when you know He has said it.

Prophetic Revelations

Our body connects with the natural realm, but our spirit connects us with the heavenly realm and we can operate in both realms at the same time. Jesus did that all the time. Because God has given you an earthly body, you have a right to be on the earth. If something happens to your earthly body, you no longer have the right to be here. Your spirit and soul will come out of your body. Our natural body keeps us in contact with the natural things here on this earth. Our spirit man is seated with God in heavenly places.

There are times when I can be driving down the road and while my natural man is looking at the road, my spirit man will be soaring in realms of the spirit, in heavenly places experiencing some things. Part of my job is to get you activated in this same thing. Some may think that is just for the prophets, but we are not talking about Old Testament prophets. We are talking New Testament prophets. Jesus literally rose from the grave and went back to heaven to give gifts unto men. What were those gifts? They were the fivefold ministry.

The fivefold are grace gifts. According to Ephesians 4:11 the fivefold are for the perfecting of the saints. Perfecting means to equip or furnish fully in the realm of the spirit.

I don't go into churches just to have services. People will come in and be content just to have a prophetic word. If I give everybody a prophetic word the first night I am there, there won't be hardly anyone there the second night. That means they don't know why I am there. It is not just to prophecy to everyone. My job is to impart prophetic mantling and anointing to the people. You don't get that with one good prophecy. You get it by coming into covenant with the prophet.

There are spiritual gifts and anointing that God imparts to the fivefold. The fivefold then imparts them to you. You may never be called to be a prophet, but you should be highly prophetic. You also need to come into covenant with a prophet to become highly prophetic. You have to walk with them, love them, understand their gift and that they are a gift from Jesus to you. When you come into covenant with a prophet, you have covenant rights. I can download everything God is giving me in time as you continue to walk with me.

It is the same way with your pastor. He can't help you if you show up once a year. *"Well, I am going through something so I am going to sit under my pastor and see if he can help me out."* When he does, then he won't see you for a year again. There are people who see their pastor that way. He is just there in case they get into trouble. But if you are walking in covenant with your pastor, he can impart some things into you that could either keep you completely out of trouble or give you that which is necessary for you to deal with that trouble and come out with victory.

I want to show you some of the reasons for prophetic ministry. Why do we need a prophet around us? Why should we have a prophet in our midst? Why should God connect a prophet to our church? Is he just a traveling minister who needs to preach somewhere?

People have asked me to come to their churches. I don't go unless I can see a covenant being built, a relationship forming so that I can be in that house enough to be of some good. Part of my ministry is to put an ax to the root of the tree. Anything that is not right I will attack in the spirit realm. In fact, I attack it just by being in the region. I can come into a region and stir up trouble because I disturb demonic spirits. It is not me doing it, but the gift of God. The Holy Spirit within me is stirring them up.

The Lord wants us to understand the purposes of the prophetic realm and why we need the prophet in our midst. In this hour we are going to see God literally connecting church after church across the nation. We are going to see churches begin to become fivefold ministry churches. Thank God for that because it is returning back to the roots of what God did in the New Testament in the book of Acts. God did not put an amen at the end of that book. It is still being written in the spirit. We are the book of Acts and we should be moving in those things. We are just now coming back to where they were in the book of Acts.

It is time to come back to the truth of God's Word, to God's church government. God has a government and it is called the fivefold ministry. When you look at the church you should not just see the pastor, but should also see apostles, prophets, teachers and evangelists. Some of them are traveling to and from, while others are in the house of God. They each have mantles and anointing that they are releasing to the body and the people are lacking nothing. They are spiritually mature, moving in the glory of God, moving in signs and wonders and miracles, moving in faith, moving in reaching the lost and touching the community. They are powerful in God.

This is what God desires to do, but we have to embrace it. We have to understand the function of the fivefold ministry gifts in order to draw from what they can give you. We are going to share some of the benefits with you from the Word of God.

Prophetic Presence

The prophets carry a prophetic presence with them. Every ministry carries their mantle anointing with them. If you are sensitive, you can feel it. Even if you don't know they are there, you can feel, sense that anointing and know they are in the building.

Several years ago Lester Sumrall was sitting on the platform in a healing and miracle campaign. The organizers wanted Oral Roberts to be with them, but he couldn't make it. Rod Parsley was sitting next to Lester, who was his mentor and trainer. The meeting was starting when Lester put his hand on his stomach. He told Rod to do the same thing and asked if he felt the anointing that had just come into the building. It was like a healing wave had just come in. Lester went on to say that Oral Roberts was somewhere in the building. They looked around, but couldn't see him. In a few minutes Oral came out and sat down by them.

I know of an apostle who will ask other fivefold ministers to sit in meetings with him. He will even pay for their motel and meals. He knows that when they come, they also carry what they have into the building and everyone will benefit from it. Mantles, anointing and gifting are beyond the flesh.

We are going to begin by going to 1 Samuel. When we see what the prophetic can do, then we can begin to draw from it.

Saul had been out looking for his father's lost donkeys. He couldn't find them and the servant with him said there was a prophet whom they called a seer. This man knew things and sometimes God would even show him where something was that was lost. They had a little bit of silver left so they went to see the prophet and take him an offering.

In that day, they knew you didn't go see the prophet empty handed. We don't understand those concepts now. It is called honor. God won't release anything through that prophet if you don't show honor. You can't buy anything though. An offering is one way you show honor.

Right before Saul showed up, God told Samuel he was coming. He wanted Samuel to anoint Saul to be king. It is interesting that sometimes when we go to see a prophet we think he is going to bring a healing to us or bring what we are looking for. Many times God will use an immediate need to get us into the meeting. The prophet may not even speak about our need. We might be concerned about our donkeys, but God is concerned about our destiny.

God knows what He is doing and He knows that the prophetic is much more than just getting your needs met, much more that meeting the immediate thing you have need of. God wants to use the prophets and the prophetic to speak about your destiny, your future, your tomorrow and impart what you have need of so that when you get to your tomorrow you have what you need to be successful in it. What good would it be to get into the future and you are not ready.

Let me tell you the formula for success. Success happens when preparation meets opportunity. It cannot be just opportunity. If you are not prepared for that opportunity, then it won't help you. Who gets hired at the time of opportunity? It is the person who is prepared for it. God wants to use the prophets to prepare us for success, for the next day, for the next thing. God is concerned about your today, but He is more concerned about your tomorrows. He knows that you need to pick up a prophetic anointing in order for you to be successful in your tomorrows. It is not just hearing a prophetic word. You have to get a mantle, an impartation, a download. You have to connect with somebody who has more than you have in order for you to get more.

1 Samuel 10:1-5; *"Then Samuel took a vial of oil, and poured it upon his head, and kissed him, and said, Is it not because the LORD hath anointed thee to be captain over his inheritance? When thou art departed from me to day, then thou shalt find two men by Rachel's sepulchre in the border of Benjamin at Zelzah; and they will say unto thee, The asses which thou wentest to seek are found: and, lo, thy father hath left the care of the asses, and sorroweth for you, saying, What shall I do for my son? Then shalt thou go on forward from thence, and thou shalt come to* *the plain of Tabor, and there shall meet thee three men going up to God to Bethel, one carrying three kids, and another carrying three loaves of bread, and another carrying a bottle of wine: And they will salute thee, and give thee two loaves of bread; which thou shalt receive of their hands. After that thou shalt come to the hill of God, where is the garrison of the Philistines: and it shall come to pass, when thou art come thither to the city, that thou shalt meet <u>a company of prophets coming down from the high place with a psaltery, and a tabret, and a pipe, and a harp, before them</u>; and they shall prophesy:"*

Isn't it interesting that the prophets have to be in the presence of God? Prophetic people have to have praise and worship. We have to get the presence of God stirred up.

1 Samuel 10:6; *"And the Spirit of the LORD will come upon thee, and thou shalt prophesy with them, and shalt be turned into another man."*

Another in this verse means tomorrow. He would be changed into his future. See what the prophetic will do for you?

Saul found himself among the company of the prophets. Saul was not a prophet. In fact, scripture didn't even say they are going to prophesy to him. It just said he would be among them and they would be coming down from a high place. That means the prophets had been with God and had been worshipping. When they came down from the high place, they were still prophesying.

If you were to get among them, you will prophesy. The same Spirit of God that is on them will come on you because you are in the same vicinity. As you prophesy, you will be changed into your future man, not who you are destined to be tomorrow.

That is what happened to Saul and he became a king. He wasn't a king before.

Revelation 1:6 says He made us to be kings and priests unto God. When we start coming near the prophetic anointing, hang around the prophets, rub shoulders with them. The word anointing or anoint in the Old Testament means to be rubbed with oil or to have oil rubbed off on you. Rub shoulders with someone who is anointed and you become anointed. It is not just about somebody ministering to you, but about you hanging out with somebody, staying around somebody, associating with somebody long enough. We become like the company we keep. There is a verse in Proverbs that says if you run with the wise, you become wise, but a companion of fools will be destroyed. So, you become a fool if you hang out with fools and become wise if you hang out with wise people. In other words, you become like the company you keep – not just someone you see every once in a while. Who are you rubbing shoulders with? Who are you associating with? Who are you connecting to heart to heart? Who are you in covenant with? Remember the prophetic amen? Who do you claim as a part of your life?

Most of you can name your pastor, but can you name your prophet? The Lord has given us apostles, evangelists, teachers, pastors and prophets. If the Lord has given us all of those, why do we only claim one? It is because of ignorance of truth. Therefore we are shorting ourselves. We are only getting one-fifth of the total anointing of Christ. Even if that minister has two different mantles on his life then we are only getting two-fifths.

We are shorting ourselves because we have not understood. Thank God for pastors with insight about fivefold ministry. Most people will say they believe in the fivefold ministry, but if you ask them who their prophet is they will tell you they haven't seen very many fivefold prophets in the earth. They will also say they haven't found anybody they think is worthy to be their apostle. It is as if the prophet and the apostle have to be more supernatural and more like God that the pastor or teacher. That is a wrong misconception. They are not more spiritual than the pastor, teacher or evangelist. It is a different anointing, a different mantle. Each one of the fivefold is as supernatural as the other.

We think it is okay to for someone to say they are a pastor, a teacher or an evangelist and we will say, *"That is great."* But if they say they are a prophet, then we say it is self-proclaimed. If they say they are an apostle, then they are high and mighty. Because of the attitude of the church, I was ashamed of what I was called to be for years. I wouldn't tell anyone until the Lord got hold of me. He asked me why I was ashamed of what He had made me. I started to tell Him, but He already knew. He asked if He had called me to be a pastor, would I be ashamed to tell someone what I was? If I were called to be a teacher, would I be ashamed to tell anyone? Would I be ashamed if I were called to be an evangelist? No I wouldn't. Then why was I ashamed that I was called to the apostolic and the prophetic? I should not let any man make me ashamed of what He had called me to be. If I am ashamed of who I am, then He will not honor who I am and the gifting will not function. I understand that some people do not like titles. If you have a title without a function then there is something wrong. Paul always said in his letters that he was called to be an apostle.

The gifting has to be there. The calling has to be there. And somebody has must be able to look at you and say you are that to them. A pastor is not a pastor unless there is somebody he is pastoring. A teacher will be teaching. In some of the churches I go I will function as a teacher, in others as an apostle and others as a prophet. That is how the people accept me. The function is there. I did not go to those churches calling myself a prophet or an apostle. They began to call me that because that is how I functioned when I was there.

I want to move in, live under and have the full benefit of the grace of God and all that Jesus provided. I want nothing that looks or even smells like religion. Religion is man's attempt to be right with God. Grace is God giving us rightness. Which one do you want? Tying to make it happen or just receiving what He already did. I would rather receive what He already did because He did it right. Religion may make somebody feel comfortable and feel like they are okay, but they aren't. They are lulled to sleep by that spirit.

Prophetic Prosperity

Can you see that Saul was changed into his future by the prophetic realm that came upon him? We can see now that we need to stay among the prophetic people, stay among the prophets and be connected to them. You need at least one prophet that you are connected to and at least one pastor you are connected to.

I want to show you something else that the prophets can do to bring you into prosperity. I have been doing it to a small degree in some of the churches I have been to. Before I can move in this I have to build a trust relationship with people. They have to know my heart, know me as a person to know that my motives are right. If our motives are wrong, then we are wrong no matter what we are doing.

Trust is built by relationship. You can't trust God until you know and have a track record with Him. God wants you to have a relationship with Him and when you do, you will come into the highest form of faith, which is trust. What is so awesome about trust is that you know no matter what happens, God is going to pull you through somehow. You trust Him to do it. All you know is God is going to see you through even though you may not know how. We have to trust Him enough to say,"*Lord, do it your way.*"

There are times when God will have you go through a very unique set of circumstances and go through a process to get your full blessing. Can you trust Him for that? I have had people come to me and tell me they had a promise about their healing, but the Lord had told them that they had to go through a surgery. I tell them to go through it then. Trust the Lord because He told them to do it. Others have come to me and said they are not supposed to have the surgery. The Lord has told them to do this and this and this. Then do it. Trust Him that come what may – the end result will happen.

God will give you the end result and you have to walk it out by faith to get there. When you are walking through it, you may think it is a hard time. If you will trust God, He will take you to the place you want to go and the end result will be everything you want it to be. There is a season and there is a reason for that season.

Sometimes in the process of going through a situation, I will pick up something I had never had before. Stuff is knocked out of me and stuff is put into me. Look at Joseph.

He had prophetic dreams of grandeur. "*I am going to be this mighty man of God. Everyone is going to bow down to me.*" Then his brothers wanted to kill him. That didn't seem to fit because Joseph saw the end result of the prophecy. Next, he gets thrown into a pit and sold into slavery. Each time it seems to get worse. He ends up in Potiphar's house and everything seems to be getting better. He's been promoted. Then Potiphar's wife accuses him and he is put in jail. All of this is happening before the end result of the prophecy.

Does it sound like your life? Thank God the end result is on the way. Start rejoicing.

2 Kings 4:1-7; "*Now there cried a certain woman of the wives of the sons of the prophets unto Elisha, saying, Thy servant my husband is dead; and thou knowest that thy servant did fear the LORD: and the creditor is come to take unto him my two sons to be bondmen. And Elisha said unto her, What shall I do for thee? tell me, what hast thou in the house? And she said, Thine*

handmaid hath not any thing in the house, save a pot of oil. Then he said, Go, borrow thee vessels abroad of all thy neighbours, even empty vessels; borrow not a few. And when thou art come in, thou shalt shut the door upon thee and upon thy sons, and shalt pour out into all those vessels, and thou shalt set aside that which is full. So she went from him, and shut the door upon her and upon her sons, who brought the vessels to her; and she poured out. And it came to pass, when the vessels were full, that she said unto her son, Bring me yet a vessel. And he said unto her, There is not a vessel more. And the oil stayed. Then she came and told the man of God. And he said, Go, sell the oil, and pay thy debt, and live thou and thy children of the rest."

There was so much blessing she could pay off all her debt because of what the prophet released over her. She and her sons could live out the rest of their lives and have all the money they needed. It was done by a prophetic word.

2 Chronicles 20:20b: *"Believe in the LORD your God, so shall ye be established; believe his prophets, so shall ye prosper."*

The Israelites did prosper. It took them three days to get all the silver and gold.

In Judges 6 we read that the Midianites and Amorites had been impoverishing the people for seven years. The people started praying. What do you think God did? He didn't send them a lot of money. He sent them a prophet. There is a part of the prophetic anointing that can break you out of poverty and break you into prosperity and blessing.

Go back to the story in John 6 when Jesus multiplied the loaves and the fish. As soon as He had finished doing that, the people said the great prophet had come. Why would the people associate the multiplying of the loaves and fish and meeting the needs of the people to the prophetic anointing? It was because they knew that was what the prophets could do.

Several years ago I was ministering in the Houston area. I handed out several pieces of cloth that had some scriptures written on them in one of the meetings. One couple came every night of the meetings. Both of them worked and they each had their own checking account. Every night they came, they would each write out a hundred dollar check and put it in the offering. Their paychecks were not large, so those checks were sacrificial.

By the way, it is not the amount of a check that makes it sacrificial. It is obedience to the Holy Spirit. You can give largely, but if you don't have the heart, the faith, are not in obedience to and following what God is saying then you are missing it. That offering will bless me, but it may not help you a lot.

When I placed a piece of cloth in their hands, I prophesied to them about the wealth that was going to come over them and about what God was getting ready to do financially. The man carried the cloth in his wallet for one year. At the end of that year, something happened. They got a check for 2.7 million dollars.

Another lady, who is in covenant with me, said she wanted some of that anointing that was on my life. It was not for her, but for a loved one. She took one of those little cloths and gave it to her brother, telling him that a prophet of God had released a prosperity anointing on it. He won almost $240,000 plus in the lottery. This man was not a Christian. She had told him that if he kept the piece of cloth on him God would release prosperity in his life.

Another couple came to us and I gave them a prophetic word. The lady began to smile. I didn't know what they did for a living, but I saw real estate. I said I saw them buying land, subdividing it and a builder, that God connected them with, building beautiful homes that she had designed. The lady grinned even more. The houses would sell as quickly as they could and at the price they were asking.

About two years later she came back to tell me that everything I had prophesied had come to pass and God had made them wealthy. They came with a check for $5,000. The couple has given that much and more in the years since then because God had prospered them so much. I told them that I saw a deal coming up with a large complex that would be offered to them. The profit would be tremendous. That deal had just been offered to them the week before I saw them.

The reason I am sharing this is because it is one mantle I carry. God wants me to release everything that is in the prophetic anointing to you.

Prophetic Creative Words

You have been created to move in signs, wonders and miracles. You have been created to be used supernaturally by God. In fact, I am going to show you that you have been created to create. I am going to share the Word of God with you and let you look at it yourself. You have the Spirit of the Lord on the inside of you.

When God breathed the breath of life into that little lump of clay called Adam that lump of clay became a living being. It became a speaking spirit, like unto God. Adam was not above God or equal to God, but was a child of God.

A part of God is on the inside of you. God breathed into Adam. The word breathed in Genesis 2:7 means to puff out or to impart spirit. God imparted a piece of His Spirit into Adam and that has been passed from generation to generation through the seed to us. That is why you are an eternal being. Your spirit and soul will live forever somewhere. It will be in heaven or hell depending on who you serve and who your God is.

You have received a portion, a piece of the very Spirit of God on the inside of you and that makes you a son of God, a child of the Most High. Your own children have a piece of you on the inside of them. They are a part of you. The same way your children and grandchildren have a part of you, we have a part of God. We are not God, though we are children of God. Our big brother is Jesus. We have the same heavenly Father.

All of that is right in the Word of God. So, why do we miss it? It is because religion wants to belittle us. A religious spirit makes us want to feel like we are nothing, nobody, worms in the dust. All of that is a lie.

There are three parts of you and God created two of them. The third one, your spirit, was imparted. Your soul (mind, will, emotions, personality)and your physical body was also created by God. Ecclesiastes 12:7 says that when you die your spirit will return to God who gave it.

In other words, God gave you the spirit that is within you. Scripture doesn't say He created it. Why is that important? In a moment I am going to show you that God created you to create. He wants you to create with words the way He creates with words.

Isaiah 48:6-7: *"You have heard [these things foretold], now you see this fulfillment; and will you not bear witness to it? I show you specified new things from this time forth, even hidden things – kept in reserve – which you have not known. They are created now [called into being by the prophetic word] and not long ago; and before today you never heard of them, lest you should say, Behold, I knew them!"* **Amplified Bible**

The hidden things – the things that God has devised for us have to do with good things.

Jeremiah 29:11; *"For I know the thoughts that I think toward you, saith the LORD, thoughts of peace, and not of evil, to give you an expected end."*

God's thoughts toward you aren't bad. He is not thinking about destroying you, not thinking about putting sickness and disease on you. He is thinking about healing, delivering, blessing you. He is thinking about your destiny and fulfilling everything that He created you to be. Those are the thoughts of God. His thoughts about you are better than your thoughts about you.

Notice the scripture in Isaiah 48 says those things are called into being by the prophetic word. The prophetic word is the word that creates.

Types of Authority

I want to show you now that Adam and Eve were given four types of authority in the garden. They lost them, but through Jesus Christ, they have been restored to us.

Genesis 1:26-28; *"And God said, Let us make man in our image, after our likeness: and let them have dominion over the fish of the sea, and over the fowl of the air, and over the cattle, and over all the earth, and over every creeping thing that creepeth upon the earth. So God created man in his own image, in the image of God created he him; male and female created he them. And God blessed them, and God said unto them, Be fruitful, and multiply, and replenish the earth, and subdue it: and have dominion over the fish of the sea, and over the fowl of the air, and over every living thing that moveth upon the earth."*

Let's start by looking at how God made man. It was in *our* image and *our* likeness, meaning the Father, Son and Holy Ghost.

God's mandate for man was to be fruitful, multiply and replenish the earth. If you want to find out what God intended, go back to the beginning.

One of the things I learned in bible study was to go back to the first mention in the bible. When you do then you will understand what the purpose of man is. It is for God to bless us. God's thoughts about you are to bless you, to do you good. There is nothing negative in that. He reserves His wrath for His enemies, not for His children. We are not destined for sickness, disease, poverty or lack. Your destiny is to be blessed so you can be a blessing. You can't be a blessing until you get blessed.

Subdue and Take Dominion

The first of the authority words is subdue. To subdue means to bring into subjection. We are to bring the whole earth into subjection. Noting is supposed to be out of order. It takes authority to restore order. Power alone can't do it. It doesn't really matter how anointed you might be, if you have no authority you really won't accomplish a lot. But, if you put the authority of God together with the dunamis power of God you will be a world changer and a world shaker.

When Jesus called the twelve disciples together in Luke 9:1-2 He gave them power and authority over all devils, to cure diseases, to preach the gospel of the Kingdom and to heal the sick. He knew that the power of the Spirit without the authority of God will not establish healing, miracles, signs or wonders in the earth.

We have to deal with order. Without order, there is chaos. There is no structure, no real life without order. Order enables life to exist and authority sets order.

God knew He had to give authority. He created man and then gave him authority.

Going back to our Genesis scripture, notice that God told them to subdue it. To subdue means to bring everything under subjection. How do you do that? It is through words just like God did.

Next He told them to take dominion. The Hebrew word for dominion mans to rule and reign.

How do you rule and reign? It is through words, by decreeing and declaring things according to the Word of God and according to what He has set up by His divine order.

In Genesis 2:15 we find the two others types of authority that was given.

Dress and Keep

Genesis 2:15; "*And the LORD God took the man, and put him into the garden of Eden to dress it and to keep it.*"

Dress and keep are authority words.

The word dress means to execute, to bring to pass, to cause to be or to make it be with words. If you don't like your garden, dress it the way you want it to be. Your life will only go the direction of authoritative words you have spoken out of your mouth. What are you saying? If you are saying that everything is bad, you are dressing your garden for bad. Don't just call things the way they are or they will stay the same. Call things that be not as though they were and they will become that way. That is how faith and words work. You call things into being and create it to be. We create thing to be the way they should be with faith, with words because we have the Word of God, the Spirit of God and the authority of God within us.

Keep is like a military term. It means to hedge about, to protect, to guard, to preserve it. How do you do it? It is with words.

God gave this mandate to mankind and expected them (Adam, Eve and their descendants) to operate in these four levels of authority. You do so with words. Adam and Eve not only lost the measure of authority they had when they sinned, they turned it over to the enemy.

Genesis 3:17-19; *"And unto Adam he said, Because thou hast hearkened unto the voice of thy wife, and hast eaten of the tree, of which I commanded thee, saying, Thou shalt not eat of it: cursed is the ground for thy sake; in sorrow shalt thou eat of it all the days of thy life; Thorns also and thistles shall it bring forth to thee; and thou shalt eat the herb of the field; In the sweat of thy face shalt thou eat bread, till thou return unto the ground; for out of it wast thou taken: for dust thou art, and unto dust shalt thou return."*

Because they sinned, the ground was cursed. That which used to bring a blessing easily now would grow thorns and thistles.

Thorns and thistles are a type of the curse. When Jesus was crucified they gave Him a crown of the curse. They drove it into his head. The moment the blood of Jesus touched the thorns, the curse was broken off the ground when it comes to us. You have to know it is broken and use your authority of the blessing.

I pastored a church in West Plains, Texas for a while. One of the farmers came to me and said he was tired of using his money to buy things to keep the bugs off his cotton. According to Deuteronomy 28 he was not under the curse anymore, but under the blessing because he was obedient to God. He asked me to come out, open my bible and spray his fields with the Word of God. I agreed.

I went out there, opened my bible to Deuteronomy 28 and spoke the blessing over his cotton and fields. I was told later that they heard me speaking out the blessings miles away. The Holy Spirit carried my voice.

The farmer took the money he would have used for insecticides and put it in the church offering. When it was time for the cotton to make, he came to me and brought a cotton boll. It was huge. He then held up another boll that came from his neighbor's field who had sprayed. It was shriveled up, eaten up by bugs. He went on to tell me that he had never had a bumper crop like that, even with spraying. We have been redeemed from the curse.

When the blood of Jesus touched the thorns on His head, the curse of poverty and lack was broken off of us. What does that mean? Now we can work without toil and be more blessed. It doesn't mean we won't have to work. We will work smarter instead of harder. We can work one job instead of four. I think I would rather be under the blessing.

Proverbs 10:22; "*The blessing of the LORD, it makes (truly)rich, and He adds no sorrow with it, neither does toiling increase it.*" Amplified Bible

What makes rich? It is the blessing. Scripture doesn't say my work will, but the blessing. What will make me rich? Will it be working a lot of hours or the blessing? You will work less, not more, because you are blessed. God working one deal for you can make you wealthy for the rest of your life.

What is toiling? It means fatigue, to be weary, to work until you are in pain, to work until you have many troubles.

Remember a story about the disciples fishing? We find it in Luke 5. The disciples had fished all night long. The bible doesn't say the worked, they toiled. In other words, they were in pain, hurting. All night long they did everything they knew to do to try and catch a fish. They went into all the places and used all of their knowledge. They knew how to catch fish and still couldn't do it. That is the curse. You think you are doing all the right things and in the natural you might be, but God is supernatural.

Jesus came along and asked if they had any meat. In other words, had they caught anything? They answered that they had toiled all night and had caught nothing. Toiling will get you nothing. It tears your body down and hurts you. Then Jesus told them to cast their nets on the other side. Jesus was telling this to fishermen, but He had a special fish finder and a fish attractor. The fish were attracted to His word.

I must tell you a story about a pastor and his wife in Arkansas. He started prophesying business for his two businesses. He prophesied that people would start calling him on the phone and wanting his services. Over the next three days they got so many calls they couldn't take all of them.

Do you want to work smarter, not harder and not toiling, but with the blessing? I want the blessing on my life.

Proverbs 18:20-21; *"A man's belly shall be satisfied with the fruit of his mouth; and with the increase of his lips shall he be filled. Death and life are in the power of the tongue: and they that love it shall eat the fruit thereof."*

A man's belly shall be satisfied with the fruit of his mouth. If you want to eat well, you must talk good. You need to prophesy stuff out of your mouth the way you want it to be instead of the way it is. If you are always speaking the way it is, you will always have it that way. If you don't like it that way, then start speaking something else. Get into God's Word, find out what you are supposed to speak and speak it.

With the increase of his lips shall he be filled. The more you speak creatively, the more you create.

Are you aware you have a treasure chest? You have a place inside of you called your spirit or your heart and it needs to be filled up with something.

If you don't have anything in abundance in your heart, what do you think is going to come out? What is in your heart in abundance will come out of your mouth in abundance. What comes out of your mouth in abundance, you will eat of abundantly. It is time to fill the treasure chest of your life with the greatest treasure of all – the Word of God.

Luke 6:45; *"A good man out of the good treasure of his heart bringeth forth that which is good; and an evil man out of the evil treasure of his heart bringeth forth that which is evil: for of the abundance of the heart his mouth speaketh."*

You have to fill your heart with good to get good. You have to fill your spirit with good to get good.

If you fill your heart with garbage, garbage will come out. Do you feel like your life is nothing but garbage? That is because all you put into it was garbage. If you are feeding on television 24/7, you have garbage in your heart. If you are feeding on the news media, you have garbage in your heart. You can feed so much on that all you have in your heart is junk.

I am putting good stuff in my heart, so that I can have good in my life. How do you program the computer of your heart? It is through your eye gate and your ear gate. David said he would put no evil thing before his eyes. Also, be careful of what you listen to. Your ears are not garbage dumps. What you hear will get into your heart and produce something. You will eat what you are listening to. Do you want good, prosperity, and healing in your life? Take heed of what you hear and how you hear. Be careful.

When you feed on the Word of God, good teaching and good preaching you fill your heart with good things and are getting prepared to create a better day with your words. We are preparing ourselves to create with words.

John 6:63; "*It is the spirit that quickeneth; the flesh profiteth nothing: the words that I speak unto you, they are spirit, and they are life.*"

Jesus is saying that the flesh doesn't profit you, and will not help you. I believe we can define flesh as the carnality of man, the fleshly desires of man. Your body is a holy thing, but our carnality brings destruction to us if we let it rule. You are supposed to rule with your spirit over your body. One of the Greek renderings for body is slave. Your body is to be a slave to your spirit and your soul. When your body gets out of control with no boundaries, no limitations and you are not ruling your body with your spirit and your soul, then you have moved into carnality and it brings destruction to your life.

These are not just the words of Jesus.

John 14:10-12; *"Believest thou not that I am in the Father, and the Father in me? the words that I speak unto you I speak not of myself: but the Father that dwelleth in me, he doeth the works. Believe me that I am in the Father, and the Father in me: or else believe me for the very works' sake. Verily, verily, I say unto you, He that believeth on me, the works that I do shall he do also; and greater works than these shall he do; because I go unto my Father."*

Jesus was saying He was going to send the Holy Spirit to help us do what He did. What did Jesus do? He spoke to a fig tree and said it was cursed because it was not producing anything. Twenty-four hours later that fig tree was dried up.

Jesus spoke to a storm, rebuked it and it stopped. He spoke peace to the sea and the sea was calm. Jesus commanded demons and they obeyed Him. He called dead people out of the grave. All of this was done with words. Jesus healed more with His words than He did with His hands.

When we were in Russia, the people were so excited that they filled the auditorium. There was no place to walk because every seat and aisle was filled with people. There wasn't even room to bring anybody to the front to lay hands on them. Half way through my message, the heavens opened up behind me and a myriad of angels started coming in. They were filling the building. The Holy Spirit began to speak to me showing me different illnesses and other things. The angels began rushing to those people and laying their hands on the affected body part. Later the people testified that they felt warm hands laid upon their bodies wherever they were sick.

This was done at a word and you can do that also. These signs shall follow everyone who believes. Scripture doesn't say these signs shall follow the prophets of God. You can have the same miracles, healings, signs and wonders that I do. Believe for it. Contend for the faith once delivered to the saints. Take hold of it. Act on it even when you don't feel it because it is not about feelings. Healings and miracles are not about how you feel.

There have been times when I didn't even feel like I had been saved while the greatest miracles were happening all around me. There were creative miracles right in front of me. I would go back to my room and weep and cry because the Lord did it. He just needed somebody who would faith it, somebody who would say it whether or not they felt it.

There have been times when the Lord told me to prophesy to someone and didn't tell me what to say. When I walked over to that person I didn't have a thing for them. The Lord would tell me to open my mouth, begin to speak and He would fill my mouth with His Spirit. That is called an oracle anointing and it takes faith.

I would open my mouth and be given a word of knowledge about something I didn't know or think of. I might be telling the person about something that happened six months ago or about an accident or something that happened to one of their kids. They might be weeping and crying while I am wondering what I had said to them. I couldn't even tell you later what it was that I said.

When you step out by faith, the Spirit of God will come upon you. Lay hands on the sick when you feel nothing and watch God do it. Sometimes I am not even sure if the person I am ministering to feels anything, but many take hold of it and might just be healed the next day. One lady I ministered to had a broken foot. She took hold of the prophetic word and overnight her foot was healed.

Are you beginning to see that the Lord wants us to create with words?

We are going to look at a time when the disciples weren't able to help in a situation. The father decided to go to Jesus because the disciples should have been able to help the man and couldn't. It wasn't because the demons were so big, but because of their unbelief. Let's read the story.

Matthew 17:16-18; "*And I brought him to thy disciples, and they could not cure him. Then Jesus answered and said, O faithless and perverse generation, how long shall I be with you? how long shall I suffer you? bring him hither to me. And Jesus rebuked the devil; and he departed out*

of him: and the child was cured from that very hour."

At a word of rebuke to the enemy, the child was cured.

Matthew 17:19-20; "*Then came the disciples to Jesus apart, and said, Why could not we cast him out? And Jesus said unto them, Because of your unbelief…*"

Notice, Jesus didn't say it was because the demons were so big and so strong that they would have to fast forty days and forty nights to gain ascendency over those devils. Even though that is not what Jesus said, it is what has been preached. We, as children of God, already have authority because of Christ. He gave us the keys of the kingdom of heaven. Whatever we bind on earth is bound in heaven. Whatever we lose, is loosed. We already have it, so what is the problem? It is unbelief.

Unbelief comes when there is too much carnality in your life. Your flesh has gotten too big and your spirit is dwindling, starving to death. You have to much of the world and not enough of God.

Unbelief means not fully persuaded. You are not fully persuaded because your eyes have been on the world, the natural, you and everything on the earth so much instead of on God and the things of the spirit. That is called carnality.

Why should we fast? It is not because the devils are so big. It is because we have some unbelief and carnality that needs to be put under through fasting. Fasting doesn't change God or the devil. It changes us so we can believe God. We already have the authority.

Matthew 17:20-21; "*And Jesus said unto them, Because of your unbelief: for verily I say unto you, If ye have faith as a grain of mustard seed, ye shall say unto this mountain, Remove hence to yonder place; and it shall remove; and nothing shall be impossible unto you. Howbeit this kind* [this unbelief] *goeth not out but by prayer and fasting.*"**

Remember, if you have too much garbage in your heart it breeds unbelief. So, what are you going to do? It is time to tone down on the things of the world and beef up on the things of God. Make sure you have some time in His presence every day. At least, give God equal time.

51350362R00040

Made in the USA
Middletown, DE
02 July 2019